The Rainbow Factory

Dear David,
Warning does not contain
rainbows !

Mark Fiddes

Mark Fiddes

Templar Poetry

Published in 2016 by Templar Poetry

Fenelon House
Kingsbridge Terrace
58 Dale Road, Matlock, Derbyshire
DE4 3NB

www.templarpoetry.com

ISBN 978-1-911132-14-1

A CIP catalogue record of this book is available from the British Library

Cover Design and Artwork by Templar Design

Typeset by Pliny

Printed in England

Acknowledgements

'The Division of Labour in Pin Manufacturing' was awarded 2nd place in the 2015 Bridport Prize.

'Agnus Dei' was commended in the 2014 Wells Festival Prize.

'The Rain in Kettering' was awarded 2nd place in the 2015 Wells Festival Prize.

'Ex.' was awarded 1st prize in the 2015 Dromineer Festival, Ireland.

'The Lost Gardens of West Norwood' was awarded runner-up in the 2013 Gregory O'Donoghue Prize and first published in *Southword* (Munster Literature)

'Tierra del Fuego' was shortlisted in the St Cross College , Oxford Prize 2015.

'Elvis Everywhere' was highly commended in the Bristol Poetry Prize 2016.

'Coarse Fishing with the President' was awarded runner up in the London Book Festival Poetry Prize 2016.

'1968 and it's all logically positive' was first published in *Queen Mob's Teahouse*.

'Time, Ladies and Gentlemen, Please' was first published in 154, responses to Shakespeare's Sonnets (Live Canon).

'Onion Music' was first published in *The London Magazine*.

'The Great Days of Tumbling' was commended in the Back Room Poets Prize 2015.

'Down Among the Shedmen' and 'My British Teeth' were both shortlisted in the Charles Causely Prize 2014.

'Freefall' was runner-up in the 2016 Ware Poetry Prize.

to Maribel, Alec and Sergi

CONTENTS

SURVIVORS

LOVERS

CELEBRITIES

EXPLORERS

SURVIVORS

THE RAINBOW FACTORY

The facts are important:
earlier today jihadi bombers fast-tracked
themselves to paradise in Brussels airport.
TV kept showing a man, his leg blown off
propped on an elbow blinking at his watch
like his flight was unaccountably delayed.
New York at Ground Zero:
the day is sunny with medium wind chill,
the pollen count high for the time of year,
mostly maple, lime and juniper.
At the 9/11 Memorial they're recycling
all the tears that ever fell and still fall,
over black slate walls in sparkling nets
though which young rainbows play
with difficulty, practicing colour like scales.
No pot of gold, just a fathomless hole.
Advisory signs say:
VISITORS ARE INVITED TO TOUCH
THE MEMORIAL NAMES PANEL.
Some stroke. Some brush. Some poke.
Some finger trace what they fear to lose
because what has a name cannot die
under this sky torn to wild blue ribbons
by all the bright new banks.
The South Tower:
with the heel of my hand
I rub and press the raised brass letters
ENGINE 6. NEW YORK FIRE DEPT.
as if there was some dumb luck in it,
celebrating neither death nor life
but the clattering ladder in between.
Back on TV, they're herding up suspects
who only lived round the corner.

THE GOLDEN AGE OF STAPLES

The Stationer takes the sun outside his shuttered door.
Dust films the geometry sets and nibs in the window.
Flash Gordonite ballpoints orbit the day-glo price stars
like a future set aside should this one fail to work.
We talk of trade, the need for rugged brown envelopes,
Jack Linsky's classic *Swingline Speed Stapler Number 3*.
He mourns the bulldog clip, put down by health and safety,
the success of the coated drawing pin over brass,
how lever-arch filing will return victorious
because humans need to feel the thickness of their lives,
refolding the facts year on tax year into A4,
to place themselves on reachless shelves or in choked attics,
mini Pharohs to the family, slaves to the Revenue.
He's kept the enamel hole punchers in his stockroom
for a parade day like this when the punters file back
from diaphanous conferencing in the iCloud.
This much he will share but only if you buy something.

THE DIVISION OF LABOUR IN PIN MANUFACTURING

MALE VOICE
I would have advised him against the ghost grey suit.
Camouflaging yourself as a dead person is hardly the look.
A male job hunter must appear spry and spear-worthy.
The tie is a sword-penis, the briefcase a box of miracles.
But he's lap-topped himself off for the day in a local café.
He's even using their plug socket. This provides cake power.
Not real power. His charts will sink and flop like sponge.
His smile will decay. He will walk as a teaspoon among men.
Nobody writes a killer pitch on a Happy Baguette napkin.
Pretending to work only makes you good at pretending.
When the family find out, he will become a jellyfish to them.
He no longer travels braced between bodies at rush hour.
Soon he will lose muscle tone, not to be trusted with the frail.
Pets will chew him like he was a toy man made of rubber
With a squeak and detachable parts that can choke a toddler.
He must return to work before his life loses interest in him.
He must visit a cashpoint to withdraw a sharp new £20 note.
He must kneel before it and kiss the profile of Adam Smith
1723 – 1790. The division of labour in pin manufacturing
(and the great increase in the quantity of work that results).
He must do this every day until work is beautiful again.
Until his next job is a magic mountain with views to die for.

FEMALE VOICE
Saturday morning, mobiles beat and gull around their bed.
Dreams, poor swimmers at the best of times, retreat under rocks.
Finding new shells, they bury themselves in wreathed pools.
Desire's jetsam bobs up before the undertow drags it down
Below a tidal bore of crocked cisterns, shot fuses and leaks.
The porn star plumber's booked but always has a better disaster.
Kids peck at the quilt to be breakfasted as her hand floats up.
Fingers lock, he reaches buoyancy for one sky blown moment.
Even now, they cannot grasp that he is drowning for a living.

MALE VOICE

Having sucked the soul from pavements and carpet tiles,
The suit grows greyer still. He is the mouse chameleon.
Far away, in a hushed and shared closet, a tie dangles.
Designed by Boss, bought by wife, strung up without trial.
The Happy Baguette works up a greasy window sweat.
Pixel-blind, his email trails criss-cross the same desert
Without answer or echo even from the Spam Viagrans.
His survival skills make a pot of spearmint tea last hours.
He smuggles wan sandwiches and biscuits from home
Where suspicions hang patient as bats from every pelmet.

FEMALE VOICE

Over an amber-swirled cup of Darjeeling, he is observed.
Under the table, a daschund worries a leg bone of chicken.
Mrs Violet Green sips and flits through her poppy red diary.
Now her dog wheezes and retches, pawing the floorboards,
Beelzebubbing from the throat, like a canine exorcism.
"Help him!" shrieks Mrs Violet Green. "Help my Victor!"
Saucers fly, the pooch is swept into a grey suited cloud,
Fingers thrust between jaws to pluck out the obstruction.
Simpering Victor returns to the tweed press of his mistress.
Strangled by its lead, the crashed laptop bleats for attention.

MALE VOICE

Mrs Violet Green will insist on nothing less than lunch.
He walks roadside followed by his faithful briefcase.
She slows for roses, topiary and artful front gardening.
A Victorian villa leans from a palisade of weeping cedars.
"Mr Green," she explains, "was a lover of the Highlands."
Through the lychgate they go, her hand a wren on his arm,
Past a granite pond, lacquered in lily pads and gasps of pink.
Milky carp slip gentle as memory through the sepia deep.
"A kinder man there will never be; all this I keep for him."

FEMALE VOICE

Look up the ladder to the pinstripe gent buffing windows,
Stretching across each pane like he's waving to a train
Departing from an upstairs room to a terminus faraway.
See the other, tailored in Empire cream linen and brogues,
Spraying the immaculate parade of guard red geraniums.
There may be others but Mrs Violet Green ushers him in
To the hallway's aspidistra chill and whiff of fried liver.
She prefers a Beethoven piano sonata with her lemon sole
As, from the conservatory, they observe the gentle minding
Of middle aged, middle managers, meddling with terraces,
Steps and lawns between statues of Gods and their quarry.

MALE VOICE

He will grasp the horseshit filled wheelbarrow of fete.
He will swell his ridged courgettes thick as torpedoes.
He will master Edwardian pipework and spidered wiring.
He will sandpaper window frames blistered with visions
Of the beloved husband's shuffling return by porch light.
He will commandeer rosters and muster the unmustered.
He will find Kant in Library time, make his life imperative.
He will perfect a backhand topspin lob in ping-pong
Leaving the Recreation Room regulars foxed and wilting.
He will see funds bubbling back monthly to his bank account
From the Mrs Violet Green Trust for Displaced Gentlemen.
He will walk home every night to a glowing family
Living each day like it was their private advertising break.

FEMALE VOICE

He will wake from winged dreams of invulnerability
To prepare crêpes with cherries for the kids' breakfast.
Quartets of patio squirrels will nibble nuts in harmony.
The porn star plumber will cosset their stroppy boiler.
A new black car will wink outside like a jewelled scarab.
Their enchanted bed will fly over minarets and moons
Through fast-drawn curtains on Sunday afternoons.

MALE VOICE
Watch. The spirits of earth and fire have stolen back
As captains who retake their citadel after crippling siege.
His tissue thickens with the quickening juju of mojo
Now working thanks to Widow Green's moneymaker.
His dark eyes that once hid under untrimmed bushes
Now glitter like starlit waters, calm before sunrise.
Around his orbit, the constellations of business align
With arrows, stings, horns, hoofs, claws and pincers.

FEMALE VOICE
Every silver cloud has a silver fish wriggling in the lining.
For Mrs Violet Green, it jiggles around her head with cancers
Until they find her lying on her bed clutching her handbag
One May morning, dressed, made-up, her dead stare stepping
Through the wedding cake ceiling to where Mr Green feathers
The eternal outboard beside their honeymoon's last mooring.
Victor snoozes alongside still believing he's going with them.
They all do, until the estate agents arrive with tape measures.

MALE VOICE
His curriculum, bursting with vitae, reads like a bestseller.
Straight backed, gold-blocked, he is 50 Shades of Combat Black,
Primed to shock and awe the Board Room with PowerPoint.
Unexploded pie charts mark the road to re-employment
Via ground-to-air word clouds and a battery of bullet points.
Fuselage white teeth say more about him than words ever can.
His breath, they note favourably, hints of mint and fratricide.

FEMALE VOICE
You don't bag the 31st floor corner office of 1 Newton Square
Without trailing scalps, bloody knuckles and redundancies.
In a resin block on the teak desk, Adam Smith smiles thriftily
From the vantage of his £20 note with City views to die for.
Victor smells fresh meat and skips from his master's lap.
A fine choice, that Beretta grey mohair with midnight silk tie.
Never fire a man unless it looks like you could kill him first.
Iced already through the frosted door, today's first victim taps.

AWRY

More intense than Jesus
he comes at me with his cup
and says fuck you
when I don't give him money.
So I call after him
holding a pound coin.
He shouts fuck you
and fuck your mother
strutting off
through the scornful traffic
like every second of him
jiggles with miracles.
He has left his smell
standing beside me;
whisky, piss and something
orange that once flowered
but never rhymed again.

LANDING AT LESBOS

"Look," she says, "a salamander."
Slipping off her father's shoulders
she skips the surf across the beach,
too nimble for the border guards.

Her creature curls around the dunes,
as orange as the fire that feeds him,
webbed in carbon black and blind
as the cola-dark sea they crossed.

Closer-up, his skin glitters
with plastic bottles, flip-flops,
flat footballs, torn sleeping bags,
a pink Barbie suitcase on wheels.

The burned tyre breath reminds her
of home, like the fat soldiers,
blind behind fake Ray-Bans,
who feed the beast more lifejackets.

DAY OF THE BIN MEN

Following a mid-Atlantic brawl,
lo-riding cyclones muscled in overnight
hurling the bins round the front yard
like they were cash-strapped junkies.

At dawn, liverish clouds scuffed past,
collars up, looking every other way
as the cadaver of our week's recycling
lay dismembered in torn white plastic.

Green lungs of glass from Rioja,
wadded limbs of sodden newsprint,
a face torn between chicken carcasses,
vegetal loins, empurpled and foliate.

Brains spilled out in final reminders,
junk mail and an unknowable cheese
that I took to be the victim's spirit
transiting from trash to paradise.

More corpses twisted along the curb,
attended now by neighbours in pyjamas
shaking their heads, waiting to be told
which terrorists we are to blame today.

PUBLIC INTEREST

Lit up like a butcher's window,
our train heaves in from the night.
Hooded paparazzi on poles look up
from grazing the platform for crime.
We are the celebrities of emptiness,
not getting divorced from each other,
or breaking the internet with our tits.
Far from strapless on red carpets
we are yachtless, beyond liposuction.
David X on the DLR invites us
to his nose picking in Silvertown.
Patti Y and her new friend celebrate
Stockwell with their sponsor Bulmers.
Karim Z sleeps all the way to Barking
after an 18 hour shift at St George's.
In veal-grey offices they cut and paste
the highlights to keep the info racy.
Somewhere a bureaucrat shudders
as he reaches his bonused target.
Arriving home we also go online
to send pictures of cats to each other,
some of them dressed as humans.

AGNUS DEI

Black as a drone,
this hawk is pure horizon.
The fields tilt. He recalibrates
the evisceration, simplified
by the lone winter star
prising light under rocks,
chasing scorpion shadows
under the dry stone fold.

The sheep all feel it.
A fear fluke makes them quiver
and stills their bleating.
Death drops quiet as lead,
straight as a pendulum slice
into the body of the lamb
spilling its ruby guts
as will become custom.

The shepherds return,
giftless, still singing the first
of many songs about the baby
born in the byre, the Easterners
and the peacock angel
they saw flaming in the skies
where now only a hawk hovers
patient and cruciform.

THE ATTRACTION OF TAXIDERMY
TO THE MODERN EYE

Some lacquer on the piano lid has blistered,
one leg chewed raw above the foot's claw.
A handful of ivories, separated like fingers,
play a diminished minor chord silently
to the empty living room which has dropped
out of tune to a century of clocks.

Landscapes hang in suet and stewed green.
Photographs of the departed queue up
on occasional tables beside the knicknackery
of widows and their crocheted whatnottery.
A Venetian chandelier floats, purple flecked
below the ceiling like a crystalised octopus.

But it's the sunlight that pulls him under
to a lake where yellow ribbons fan the walls
as if through weeds, over furred stones.
He faces the pike in its case on the mantel,
pending with menace over the fake shale,
scales as rusted as an armoured Assyrian.

Saw teeth bared, one thunderous eye
has him trapped between velvet swags,
porcelain spaniels and limp aspidistras.
The mirror over the fireplace throws back
a man who has mastered the art of waiting,
gasping lungfuls of stale hyacinth.

DIRTY MAGIC

Headlong, the storm horses roll in,
ratting the shutters like fast rosaries,
black as printer's ink, shaking loose old prayers,
mares not of night but a furlong beyond.

New lovers lock, each body softening
after the rush, just to cling to something.
Others sigh alone, stranded in their beds,
dreams scattering over the flats like crabs.

This is what it's like to be back at war
thinks the old man, brewing another pot,
not for the first time since midnight struck
in his tea-sweet house of books and boxes.

All this dirty magic, he's seen before:
conjured causes and escapology
as trap doors open and sons disappear
to canned applause carried off on the winds.

Far away, in a temple-strewn desert,
the plague of bombs spreads from terrorist cells
to hospitals where war is the only work
fit for men too chicken to show their face.

Closer by, the dead lie flat in their best
thrumming the soil with that familiar grin
waiting for the comfort of younger friends
once the wild-eyed night has turned tail.

PATIENTLY

We wait
as 70's hits spit into the butter yellow room,
lost in France with Bonnie Tyler and Oncology.
We wait
with the O'Connors, the Koslov's and Ibrahims,
bar coded, pre-loaded into buff sprung folders.
We wait
as if waiting were our new job in plastic chairs
dusted with urine and its close relatives.
We wait
Wondering if there's method in the madness
of male pattern baldness or if it's just chemo.
We wait
eying the ashen portakabin past the window
for evidence of human tea-drinking or filing.
We wait
for apologetic mispronounciations of our names
like we were ambassadors of lost languages.
We wait
while the orderly wheels the man who folds
with a wheeze along the corridor.
We wait
all of us clocks in the slow process of stopping,
hoping for angels to reset the tender mechanism.
We wait
for someone to take down the Christmas decorations.

THE TERRACE AT THE END OF THE WORLD

I live in a fragile house
Rain blisters the windows
Wind wolfs at the casements
Doors burst into their frames
Electricity surges like a wildcat
Scratching out filaments and fuses
Gas sleeps rough in Victorian corners
The boiler chokes and heaves like a keeled beast
With its burden trodden into the muddy road
Beside which we freeze, refugees from sleep
Awaiting the milkman's sodding whistle
That at any other dawn would mean
Execution by a drunk firing squad
But today signals the all clear
Even if it's Lloyd -Webber
He twitters, a distant hit
From *Cats* or *Les Mis*

THE RAIN IN KETTERING

This sky is a professional
on loan from East Anglia
or some other official region
with its own BBC News
and school of landscape art.
All afternoon it has sucked
the shadows from under our feet
up into its black yawn,
suspending us in air so thick
it might contain the grindings
of another non-league town
as mild and brickish as our own.
Splashes now land like hot kisses
tasting of stale meat and steel.
The first drops fritter onto laurels
in globs and splats and rills
over butts and pots and sills.
Retirees flee into conservatories,
stricken as citizens of Gomorrah,
with pails and copies of The Mail
rolled into truth truncheons
against the great wet reckoning.
Civilians stand ceremoniously
under hammered bus shelters
still as Britain's many rain dead
while hoody loons turn cartwheels
in Wicksteed Park, ditch-giddy.
All the kids wish to be tumbling fish
wondering if we were Eskimos
how many words we'd give to this.
Just as suddenly the artillery stops.
New mud rises, blinks from drains.
The guttering of Kettering breathes.
Its honeysuckle declares world peace.

THE MUMURATIONS

An Amaretto paper cylinder
burns into a witch
and flies towards the window.

A scythe of earth
hooks under a thumbnail,
gritty as salt.

Oil scabs the beach
where a slick gull stares
with ceramic eyes.

The cloak of starlings
unspins over a corded field
revealing dusk.

A broken moth drums out
a refrain of dust
against the plastic lampshade.

Smoke coils
from the charred tail-wick
of a birthday cake.

This pimpled leak
on the bedroom ceiling
goes from kidney to lung.

A fuzzy new star
makes an appearance
on this morning's X-ray.

THE PERSONAL EFFECTS OF DON ESTANISLAO

When they are gone
they leave chairs in attitudes of conversation
while the words shuffle off to another room.
Only his silhouette stays, etched over decades
in light upon velvet, a still life with El Pais,
toothpicks and toffees lost between cushions.

The shutters are worn out
with looking beyond the far fields that dissolve
into milk through the copper lip of trees.
His thumb has rubbed down the brown gloss
to a keen patch of grain, whorled like an eye
keeping watch from the wood.

Perhaps you know
of a charity shop that will take the shepherdesses
boxed up in the hall with their porcelain swains?
Somewhere there's a silent family that needs
a wall of encyclopaedias from 1972 (volume K
pressing a gardenia to its heart).

The dial has broken,
so long has he tuned the bedside radiogram
to that station, short-waving like him
between Hilversum and Madrid, twitching
with static and meds as the military bands
tramp along behind, warless and triumphant.

THE LADYBIRD BOOK OF CANCER

There should be a technique,
there always is, for yogi and poets
to visualise exterminating all death spores
before any shock and awe surgical strike
or pressing the nuclear therapy button
to blast out the bad cells like Pacific atolls.
In my guts I pictured pissed-up Hemingway
hooking tumours like blue fin tunas
from a speedboat jiggling with bikinis.
Lung deep, Larkin could pick them off
like flies with a rolled up railway timetable.
For anything problematic and pancreatic,
Elizabeth Bishop might stare it out,
slice it up and offer it to her cats.

I never imagined the Taliban
holed up darkly between balls and arse,
bristling testosterone terrorism.
What if the boss of hospital ops fails
and I'm laid out in a box for England
to flavour this land that nourished me?
Slip into the casket my original muses
Spring, Summer, Autumn and Winter
from Ladybird's 'What to look for' series;
lambs suckling blossom from the thorn,
the tractor's doze beyond the dog rose,
a leaf-red squirrel misering in the mists,
the heron's reedy sermon to an iron dawn.
Let's all turn book worms under the sheets.

ON THE NAMING OF TUMOURS

Blonde, entitled, bursting with ambition,
my MRI scans through his candidacy,
already too grand for the gland he has chosen.
"Hello Boris," I say.
There he sits without jokes or the zipwire
they should have sliced to be done with him.
My personal Boris with his will to power
over a body we had always managed pretty well
as an anarcho-syndicalist cooperative.

"Musn't grumble," the guts would nod back
when challenged with vindaloo or goat tagine.
"To each according to his need," the heart cried
and who among us would have disagreed?
"Let 1000 flowers bloom!" proclaimed the eyes
who we all loved, believing every painted word.
"Il faut épater le bourgoisie!" charged the brain
who forever appeared to be one step ahead of us
despite the langauge problem.

So we hotline crack Urologists to infiltrate
under cloak of darkness, through the backstreets
with blades, robots and extreme prejudice.
Next day, official reports confirm his removal
to a tray somewhere for further interrogation.
Not that we're expecting a sincere apology.
They can't repent, they're only tumours.

LOVERS

Ex.

She waited for the eclipse to dump him.
It felt right with her light so hidden
for so long by so changeable a man.
She slipped orbit outside Caffè Nero
on the Victoria Station concourse
after buying him a full fat mocha.

Soon the solar shadow closed over them.
Southern Rail pigeons drifted widdershins
in slow-motion as if underwater,
like the man, turning tie-less on the spot,
upper lip frothed with milk and she wondered
if she'd have loved him more with a moustache
or a dog, or a dangerous hobby.

Kissing him on the ear, she moved off
with the wave she plucked from her handbag
through the barriers to Platform 12
where down the tracks the sun spilled back
like the opening credits in a dark cinema
beyond Selhurst, Woodmansterne, Brighton
and all stations south to her sea with no tides.

THE LOST GARDENS OF WEST NORWOOD

Spring has not been a great success
in the claylands of South London
now daubed in dog shit fauvre
and splashes of sepsis yellow.
May's the cruellest month on record,
even the crows have lost interest.

"We are now approaching Balham"
Southern Rail announces
without sympathy or respect.
Weary sheds and flailing trellis,
early cabbage and sacks of woe
spilling bottles to Streatham Hill
where late commuters goggle eyed
wait outraged as stranded salmon.

The lost gardens of West Norwood,
buried many Edens deep in
a conspiracy of ivy and knotweed
yield the flotsam of childhoods past:
plastic chairs and cricket bats,
the slow rusting barbeque
that carbon dates the happiness
of a long divorced family.

In the drizzle of Gypsy Hill,
pale mansions damp with memory
dissolve gently as pain-killers
into the moss-choked guttering.
We shunt on to Crystal Palace
twinned with Melancholia,
a murder scene with brick arches
and ornamental dinosaurs.

Behind the sweating café glass
a man holds his lover closer
than a cello, breathing her hair
for the first bowed note of summer
while on we roll to London Bridge,
their kiss blooming deep within us.

MORE LAUNDRY

Shortly after crawling
you started to leap the stairs
like the house was on fire
which often it was.

You bared every thread
on the edge of the last step
so now a tread grins through
frayed cord and superglue.

On the sofa, you coiled up
with laughter that fossilised
in cushions stiff with dust
and the sediments of us.

Years of TV bickering
misted the handset numbers
so we made a braille for males
to help us find our highlights.

You're packing up your laundry,
rolled, folded neat as dough
into the back of your Polo
home to your student bombsite.

Later, behind stale curtains
I will hear you calling out
high up in another tree
from a different garden

like you can't climb down:
Dad,
Dad,
like I can't climb up.

Son.

PROFIT AND LOSS

Twin mowers strim the cemetery
at a fair lick circling the graves
for a final short back and sides
before winter clippers in.

In bone white tufts, toadstools pop up
like word bubbles from comic books,
speechless at how well death is done
up here, above the churn of worms.

The buzzing stops, bird song returns.
An employee in green fatigues
hangs his football cap on the head
of a stone angel, her wings tucked

like van Eyck's Annunciation
without the rainbows or tidings,
an earthly representative now
not of God but Big Sam Allardyce.

At her feet, he sits to eat his roll
to sip a Coke, to pick his nose,
to count sun-trapped stuttering bees,
to read the fond gold inscriptions.

I close the year's ledger on this
scribbled slip of light, to forget
those days of loss that slid away
beyond our feint blue margins.

DES RES

We've not seen the man at Number 7
since his hedge blossomed pink
and spring sauntered in with Death
in its buttonhole, wafting hyacinths.

Mourners pass through the rusty gate,
its magpie scrape welcoming
the Hyundai full of young adults
with soft beards, Oakleys and saris.

The mother unravels up the path,
a scream simmering behind her hand -
lifted by the same arms she had jabbed
against Britain's rash contagions.

In her wake glide the radiant tupperwares
of cake, gulaab, sandesh, modak , jalabi,
all winged down with lotus blessings
from the paradise kitchens of Mitcham.

A grandson returns from his hatchback
with a can of WD40, sprays the gate,
hinges, springs, swings it both ways,
catches the drips in a white hanky.

The men file inside, their silence as worn
as their rubber soles, past the SOLD sign
foretelling the advent of a hedge fund guru
with ambitious plans for the basement.

PRESERVES

If I tipped the jamjar
to the lips of the wind
they would purse and flute
the song of every bird
heard along the valley.

If I caught the March sun
inside I could unwind
its twig light into flags
flying coloured fanfares
over the biscuit fields.

If I swung it across
the trout stream I could skim
a mist of spawn and weeds
to capture the flame breath
of sapphire dragonflies.

If I dragged it over
the far boundary rope
I could muster linseed,
raw turf and the chugging
of summer's secret lawns.

If I had lidded this
and labelled every year
you might spoon up the fruit,
tart and sweet, of exile
with no hope of return.

ELDERFLOWERS

You showed us how to prove love was true
even in wintertime by holding a snow drop
to your wrist so it would glow like a pearl.
The bloom now lies just under your skin,
roots tapped into losses and brown mercies,
budding violet and petalled under the eye,
a rash of rose and fuschia asters threading
down the cheek, matching slurred lipstick,
the daisy stare after your sundowner meds,
a general tendency to magnolia in all things.
A new scent teeters between pee and lillies
as your hands flutter like cabbage whites,
lavender veins too close to flowering again.

SAFETY PROCEDURES #7

As words are such liars,
I made us a translation box
from jewellers' cases, cigarette packs and wine bottles.
I stretched stockings over fancy woks for speakers.
To cover up the flaws, I tore pages from beauty magazines.
Powered reliably by domestic friction,
it never broke down.

For a while
I was convinced I could hear you faithfully
until the only phrases that cut through were saw-toothed.
So I clipped on holiday snaps and kids' toys for kindness
with mirrors to foresee any orders coming down the line.
One day, in my panic,
I tripped and smashed it to pieces.

Only then,
I recognised I had become invisible,
haunting my own trashed apparatus,
making a recurring click, looking for a light switch,
forgetting I'd blown the fuses years ago.

ONE AMBER DAY

Imagine instead, a decade ahead
the sun still spills over your skin.
You fizz a little inside your clothes
and the arm around you is mine.

Here your troubles are trapped
like a bluebottle fly in amber,
an exoskeletal compression in light
to exhibit on lingering afternoons.

You sneak a peak before I slide it
back into the specimen drawer
with all the other creepy crawlies
that sparkle more with age.

ELBOW ROOM

In this...your bum looks neither big nor small.
It is beyond size by which I mean just perfect
which is to say you could have worn anything
and the effect would be stunning. Not that you would
just wear anything, having such amazing taste in all things.
Indeed, any backside would be fine as this isn't objectification
based on the standard male gaze but on empirical observation
made by female friends with good science degrees. I might as well
have remarked on another most deserving body part but having
fantastic elbows might be taken euphemistically, despite both
of them being beyond conventional measurement, redefining
their significance solely as attributes to your core essence,
your "you-ness", your *Wesensheit*, your real self.
Like your buttocks.

VENUS ATTACKS!

You would expect an announcement
to prepare for full-on alien invasion,
voiced by the tannoy God of lampposts
or a dickie-bowed newscaster recorded
in the age when the best-laid catastrophes
wore gas masks and had their own midnight.
Some emergency sirens might have been nice,
although they're nothing new round here.

The morning sky had been dialled down
to low, corrugating over the city roofs,
air too thick for wing or web or song,
heat pooling from the cracks and manholes.
Even the ants exporting our sugar efficiently
all summer stayed nested under their slabs.
Then it appeared, bobbing over the fence,
trailing a streamer, looking to see if we were in.

Just its big red heart balloon head,
bobbing and trailing towards the back door,
over the step, as if it knew its way around,
hestitating for a glance around the kitchen,
then toppling off towards the mothy sofa
where it sank, exhausted after its Odyssey
through the blackest holes of deepest space,
all the way back home.

TIERRA DEL FUEGO

When you go home again
you leave your country
mapped out on the bed
in folds and quiet valleys,
bordering a desolation,
exposed, frozen, eroded,
your personal Patagonia
where tongues spoke fire
and love made monsters.

Me, with my two heads
emerging from the forest
where you left me Emperor.
By your warrant I decree
the burning of cartographers
to preserve our terra nova
and its tectonic sheets,
to leave rivers impenetrable,
the timbers un-burgered
and every peak flagless.

Tonight, in window seat 10A,
you rattle your gin and tonic
watching the shimmer below
grow vast into your city,
hot with beats and carnival
while I lie awake in a coat
listening to glaciers
and the cats at it again.

WHAM!

The mosquito has left a map
on the magnolia wall,
a foreign country etched
school atlas red in blood,
bordered with scraps of wing.
The rolled up Heat magazine
remains pristine even where
Kim Kardashian took the hit,
her fake arse fatal in my hands.

There was blood earlier too
chasing round the sink basin
like a Chinese dragon
staining our silken tooth floss
the colour of luck or money
swirling counter-clockwise
back to the Equator
with a serpentine gurgle
that left the hotel plumbing
shuddering past lunch.

Up the broken lift shaft
we hear bar chanticleers
crowing for cocktails and pints
from the hip studded lobby
some happy landings below us.
We will join them for slammers
and still-pink ribs with chips
then fold back into our sheets
flat as missionaries' charts
inked with fresh expeditions.

FREEFALL

She takes him up to the 32nd floor
in London's hard money district
to celebrate the big day at a restaurant
significantly closer to Heaven.
The protuberances of high finance
poke through cloud, chrome-ribbed:
the cigarette lighter, the vibrator,
the Ladyshave, the vast dictaphone,
all the naff caboodle of an 80's playboy
or some gargantuan James Bond
who's just tossed the lot away.
Vertigo zip wires from his calves
to his gut to the sirenscape below
as they toast the Anniversary.
She's the one with a head for heights.
For him, it's the perfect altitude
for another assisted crash landing
while she circles over the big stuff:
kids, house, holidays, hormones,
the lack of public hand-holding.
THE COMPLETE FAILURE
TO HOLD FUCKING HANDS.
The Szechuan signature dishes
undress in his shuttered mouth
but none of the words will come.
Eastwards, along the brown river,
brass cymbals of sunlight crash
over mansion blocks and stadiums,
carparks, markets and stockyards,
over all the choked roads that head
everywhere but to this ledge.
He presses his palm into hers.
Their fingers steeple to a summit.
A thousand feet up, his life still beats
to every breathless second of her.

THE THEREMINS OF ID

This morning the chorus
dissolved into sediments,
pouring fog round corners,
over iron-bladed lawns.

The dream circus moved on.
All the lead trapeze artists
fell tangled into spiders' webs
hanging from damp hedges.

The clown car of desire
crashed into the lion's cage
while the tamers were off
on a well-deserved vacation.

The oom-pah band of ego,
the massed theremins of id,
packed up their instruments
leaving just this sheet music.

I should really let you sleep
but if I kiss you wide awake
you'll accuse me of teasing
when all I have to show is mist.

SKIN GEOMETRY

She had this other mouth.
A wrist line, razor straight
that had long healed over,
unresolved as a calculation
in chalk which I followed
with my crude thumb,
being bad at mathematics.
She stared either side of me
like I had opened a window
to a whirring scented night
that had to be dreamed though.
"They called it a cry for help,"
she said, while that summer
it was her bigtime crimson
Declaration of Independence
rippling across the warm gulf
to her prayerful parents.
I felt irresolute, as we all do
meeting true revolutionaries
who are famous, not to crowds
but to themselves, welcoming
the currency of tourists
with kind arms and mix tapes.

ARMISTICE NEAR ARBECA

Following an argument
we go to look for war graves
among stunted olive groves
spindled in mist and rumours
of a quiet atrocity.
Below power lines of crows
discordantly scored like staves,
winter has many silences
to which we add another.
Hunting for spent munitions,
we interrogate the land
with sullen boots and prodding:
rusted caps of Cacaolat,
Japanese pornography,
a shrunken red wool mitten,
a Citroen's twisted wheel hub,
shuffled bones of carrion,
a shivering grey condom,
the ghost of love that slipped away
not so long before own own.
Later we make food for hours.
James Bond's on Telecinco.
Hands regain their gravity.
With one kiss we both agree
not to speak of it again.

A GOOD DAY FOR STUNT MEN

Budget flights roar back from paradise
ripping the sky above us open
like a fat, white envelope
stuffed with nothing much,
no gods, no promises or jackpots,
only clouds rag rolling off to Essex.
"A good day for washing"
they would have said over the fence
in the century before tumble dryers.
We watch
as cabin crews prepare for landing,
all digital devices are switched off
and seats returned to upright positions,
dusted in the same milk sun
that makes stains of our shadows
faint as breath on the paving
where the late nasturtiums
turn from flame and chrome yellow
to tiny fists of rust.
We think about going indoors,
maybe there's mail or a message,
or just staying put,
in case a bright stunt biplane
trails a banner telling us "It's alright.
Everything's going to be OK."

CELEBRITIES

ALL OUR BENEFACTORS

Stone virgins slide between sheets of rain
in parks and graveyards as the taxi speeds
back for a mild domestic urgency.

In the wildly pedestrian precinct,
the bashed steel shutters of a betting shop
clatter open for the early vodka jockeys.

The concrete fountain now dribbles verdigris
turned on the same year as *La Dolce Vita,*
when what they needed was Anita Ekberg.

Sun hides in the hole through the Henry Moore,
donated when hope was worth paying for,
before the omnivorous Mall landed.

As planners thought only in roundabouts,
all roads cross at humps named after Lord Mayors
shaped like the tumuli of pigmy cheiftans.

To the last estate, where that red in the bricks
will never heal and curtains flick uncertain
as to where all this grit keeps falling from.

ELVIS EVERYWHERE

My first Elvis was Chinese,
Jade Palace, Old Kent Road.
He made a hen party of us all,
his joylucky thrusting, sideburning
the joint in a white hot jump suit.
Only a microphone kept him alive
above the faraway tide of
Are you lonesome tonight?
as hollow as a fortune cookie.

Welsh Elvis was the real deal.
He sneered out *Hound Dog*
prop forward lips burst as crackling
at a wedding in Aberystwyth
where knickers flew in thanks.
Later at a howling bus stop
we found him feeding pigeons
with sausage rolls and vol au vents
he'd sneaked out in his wig.

There's only one Munich Elvis.
He does *Wooden Heart* online
with hand actions like a marionette
varnished with Hawaiian Tropic.
The bio says he works for BMW
and loves to water ski with friends.
He's married to Priscilla who runs
the Malibu nail bar off Karlsplatz.
He takes all major credit cards.

Homeless Elvis is Mr Showbiz.
He sleeps around Charing Cross
but comes from Govan via Basra.
Every evening his masterquiff rises
beyond the reach of mortal comb,

whorled and tapered like a unicorn,
dazzling with Brylcreem and starlight.
He never sings but his cardboard sign
says *Viva Las Vegas*.

COARSE FISHING WITH THE PRESIDENT

"Why the bare chest Mr Putin?"

Behind us, salmon bounce the falls
sideways, backwards, upside down,
flipping as if the rocks were sizzling.
He's giving me that whipped dog look.

You must feel the sun upon your heart.
It is Russian sun so it makes you strong
like a bear or a city or a larch.

Anti-machismo snow starts to fall
in big doily cake shop flakes
fading on his oh-so-tattoo-able torso,
slippery clean as a hard-boiled egg.

The salmon now vault like acrobats
in harlequin jackets flashing on and off.
Putin slips down his camouflage fatigues
to silver underthings, legs like trees.

In Russia, our fish don't swim,
they dance. All animals dance by law.
Even our donkeys and foxes.

Now we're at the abyss, how will he fish?
A rod and fly, maybe strangulation?
A couple of grenades would do the job
although crossbow is more his style.

But it's too late. A spiked fin protrudes
from his chest and rainbow scales glitter
around his neck and scalp. His feet
rib out into a mottled fan.

The President of the Russian Federation
scythes through the thundering spume
to gavotte around a pink bellied sockeye
who Merkels back with quivering gills.

JOCKY WILSON SAYS

If I made it as far as Purgatory
I'd swap Virgil for Jocky Wilson,
dark-locked Achilles of the dart.
Unlike Eros and the other Gods,
he knew what he was throwing at,
holding the present moment
like a silver quivered space shot
bound for the centre of the universe
or its outer limits, quitting the oche
with a who-gives-a-flying-fuck
acrylic strut through the gloom
to a temple of pints and chasers
wreathed in delphic Rothmans.
Now in Paradise, all they talk about
is how many angels fit on the tips
of Jocky's tungsten arrows.

1968 AND IT'S ALL LOGICALLY POSITIVE

Beige fabric drapes the TV studio in strips of lightning.
Our philosopher imp sits on the sofa twinkling and smoking
in unassailable tweeds and a cravat the colour of poison.
An interstellar chrome ashtray hovers alongside, co-starring.
His philandering eye moistly winkles out the researcher
with clipboard and specs who might yet be an ex-student
before the interviewer slow bowls a new question of decent length.
The philosopher reels off Schlick, Carnap, Frank, Feigl, Neurath,
Gödel and Bergmann like they were the seven dwarves of logic
to his Snow White, co-causing an eyelash flutter at the girl floating
beyond the cables and spotlights in the pink knitted twinset.
Next he tackles Ethics, rattles some matches from his pocket,
lights up again, produces smoke, like he's charcoal burning sticks
of Truth from raw Nature, telling the War Century's great secret
that Morality is nothing more than Oxbridge for Being Bossy.
Then catching himself on a monitor, he identifies transcendence
(a transmission of pure sense data projected onto a colour cloud
meaning he will never be more real than this, even in a future
where nothing will exist until televised and modern philosophers
will be pop promoters, gossip queens and cheeky banterists).
The interviewer ends on a shuttlecock knocked up for a smash:
"So thinking back to the Vienna years, what image comes to mind?"
The galactic ashtray intercepts a last fag as the philosopher quips:
"A signpost saying *Wien*."
Irritatingly, he has never heard signs talk, but only one truth counts:
the minx with notes chewing the pencil behind Camera 3
who will shortly accompany him through the press of technicians
to the place that is neither green nor wholly a room at the same time
for Scotch on the metaphorical rocks and the possibility of peanuts.

TO MARIA CAYETANA DE SILVA,
THE 13th DUCHESS OF ALBA

Your Grace,
I will require you to wear black which will move under my paint
because your enchantment is never still.
I ask that your red scarf drapes around your waist like a general
returning from war against an old enemy.
I will place you under a southern sky the blue of birds' eggs
on common ground where hunters and thieves might stalk.
A path will wind between bushes lightly stroked as if in early mist.
You will stand not as a duchess but a dancer of the Tarantella
with the air itself parting in applause.
On your visit to my studio you said I reminded you of a cat
leaping across rooves between sleepers and their dreams,
slipping on starlight and using my brushes for balance.
Let me lift you above the crows and winged hauntings of your grief.
I will frame you for as long as watchers choose to wonder.
In return you will point to the earth under your gold silk shoes,
to one name,
Solo Goya.

The portrait was started shortly after the death of her husband the Duke of Alba in 1796.

7 DAYS

It's snowing David Bowie
one humdrum Sunday later.
Slow ashen clown drops
unsettling everywhere
over South London.
Death's the kabuki next door
with its masks and mime,
its dark carpet demanding
you scatter more stars
so the end makes sense
which it will if you're there
standing by the wall.

KING OF KRILL

"We have a novelist,
a humourist, a politician,
a publicist, a broadcaster,
a painter, a poet,
even a shrink..." said Sigmund,
"What we truly need...
is a decent *Fischhandler*."
"You mean Fishmonger, Uncle.
Let me make you one."
Over the next twenty years
there extended a Freud
straight of spine, strong of wrist
cold of eye, cord fingered.
Apprenticed to a Guildsman,
he aced his studies,
parsed groupers from snappers,
became the toast of Billingsgate,
opened a gut-your-own eatery
in Soho for hipsters,
DJ'd sushi in Bouji's,
MC'd a Fish-co-teque
at Glastonbury,
launched on Sky Living
The Fish Channel,
reinvented chips,
joined Richard Branson in space,
conquered America,
created Krill King,
the first fast fish chain
until world stocks ran out.
Retired to Hampstead,
accused of codnapping
the last batch of roe
and hatching them
in his private swimming pool,

changed his name to Smith.
Opened a nail parlour in Braintree,
called it Electra's,
sold up, played golf,
disinherited,
died happily, curled fetally
in a nice warm bunker
on the tricky 16th.

THE RHYME OF THE MORRIS TRAVELLER

The half-timbered car appeared overnight
as if abandoned by some Tudors on a day trip
to Streatham to check out the state of heresy.

Hunched between ripped Baltic super-legends,
British gumption had leaked from its chassis,
streaked and lumped as Sunday gravy.

Disgruntlement lipped the radiator grill
like the moustache of Sixties Labour Minister
with a grudge in need of a pipe and a good shag.

Come lunchtime, the Borough Parking Stasi
had wadded a ticket under its flimsical wipers
sidling back to their bunker under Town Hall.

Given all the recent Magna Carta palaver,
I took the warrant into my own hands for scrutiny,
complete in each detail, except *Colour: Unknown*

When it should have read *Colour: Coventry*
or *Cowley* where the factory palettes were inspired
by classics from the Great British Breakfast.

Sausage brown Allegros, fried tomato Talbots,
smoky bacon Princesses, eggy Hillman Imps,
and the baked bean Mini with mushroom trim.

When the clamp crew hauled up with their crane
perched on the truck like a day-glo pterodactyl,
I waved the docket, channelling Gregory Peck.

"Everything has a colour," I said clear as Atticus.
The buzz-cut geezer in the florescent vest
pressed the winch button with a Clinty squint:

"Maybe…but not every colour is knowable."
For the first time, the Morris Traveller ascended,
smiling between bumpers like the Queen.

BEST SUPPORTING ACTOR

As you're talking cult movies,
I'd have my soul played by
Robert De Niro driving a taxi
with a gun in the fridge.
At night he smothers his traffic flow
with a pillow.
In the morning he helps old ladies
with their shopping.
He says his girlfriend is performed
by Scarlet Johanson
but nobody's ever seen her
so we call her Secret Chanson.
He's smoother now
as bits of him have rubbed off
in other people's houses
except that black beauty spot.
His theme tune is Greensleeves
screamed from a Marshall stack
the way Hendrix stripped bare
The Star Spangled Banner.
He reads only sequels
like The New Testament,
Skinhead 2 and Proust.
Daily, he waits for someone to yell
"Cut! It's a wrap!"
so he can make it back to his trailer
for a happy ending
in his crepe-soul brothel creepers.

FRA ANGELICO GLIMPSES ETERNITY

(on the San Domenico Altarpiece)

After Purgatory, there's no wheelchair access.
Between circles of heaven, the escalators crowd
with Dominicans, martyrs, saints and bishops,
ermine trimmed in top Florentine toggery.
Across God's Mall, their faces gleam, coins of flesh,
eyes narrowed on the Redeemer in a white throw.
He's handing out benedictions like there's a sale on.
The seraphim security detail look too smooth,
modelling an anti-aging secret that's only available
to subscribers of the celestial shopping channel
while the putti have been gunning milk shakes and fries
and the aircon is pumping the kind of divinity
that gives you a sore throat and that bloated feeling.

Fra Angelico waits for the varnish to dry.
Already two days late, he's skimped on the gold leaf.
There will be hell to pay from the authorities.
Or maybe there won't. Not yet.

EXPLORERS

THE PRICELESS GIFT OF TWEED

I will always regret the hat
I did not snap up in Bridport,
lilac flecked and rough as heather
storked on chrome legs in the window.

Destined to be my pub helmet,
it was to guard against SKY News,
lads on the lash and men with dogs
always quoting The Telegraph.

Maybe a Dorsetter sports it,
striding along the chesil tide
with a pink child past fossil walls
skimming stones like calcium birds.

Or a Japanese scholar sits
still as a pot in a zen garden
sensing the itch over his scalp
wondering why it feels like rain.

Hopefully, it shades a cowboy
dapper and lonesome on a peak
above a peachy Utah gulch
surveying the final stampedes.

I know I should have sacrificed
that crap takeaway and bought it,
as my memory would be better
with that hat to keep it fresher.

ONION MUSIC

I grow lighter for you
with each striptease
from skin to skin leaving
a glimmering bulb
a milk light by your bed
for you to undress by
or find your way to the loo.
I remind you of your births
with this universal belly
its faint meridians stretched
drum tight and kicking
without howls or rips
offering only the stillness
learned from warm earth.
Put me on your dresser
I will be your hope grenade
pinless among magic sticks
and brittle bottled miracles
reminding you to forget
the drip of years and live
each day like it was your first.

DAS LIED VON DER ERDE
(at the Anselm Kiefer retrospective,
the Royal Academy, London)

A butcher's field, not a farmer's.
Unhealed furrows scar the canvas,
salved with the ashes of telephone directories.
Your air hangs loose as chicken skin, its sun a comb seared.
This is where
they disappeared.

The Nuremburg forest. Christ, Hitler, You
(delete as appropriate) doing the old Seig Heil
in your dad's army greatcoat on the gash-raw bank
of a filthy river, watched by the trees, swart, uncleared.
This is where
they disappeared.

Black sunflowers,
each neck broken on your flesh stalks.
Metal seeds scatter the soil like bullets or filled teeth.
At least Van Gough kept the blitzen between his ears.
This is where
they disappeared.

At the exit
I hand back the audio guide.
Your Song of the Earth is still so loud
as ravens wheel across the thresher's steer,
even the narrator's voice
has disappeared.

NAMASTE

A Victorian snug
hugger-mugger with yoga mats.
A waxy peace
moon candled for jaded chakra.
A downward dog
arses for heads, chi trip-switching.
A light lunch
mere lentils and rice, half a Twix.
A distant snarl
faraway lion on the Savannah.
A grizzling
rival prides circle over an ibex carcass.
A whine
the jackals have caught on.
A rumble
who invited the elephants?
A screetch
descent of the gut monkeys.
A stampede
warthogs, rhinos, wildebeest, zebra, antelope and…
Thunder
harken, the many-sphictered Zadok, high priest of methane
and relax
around me the lycra sylphs - still alive - twitch and stir.
A child's pose
Namaste

THE GREAT DAYS OF TUMBLING

You
were a barrel
of myths rolling
down Glastonbury Tor
jangling up Fata Morgana
and Jagger. Lime leaves flickered
quick as grass snakes slipping through
the dawn Mendips where the sun yolked
the sky like a great fried breakfast. Pickled
Merlins haunted every pub, tawny pints as wise
as owls perched in their grip. Here you bundled in
munching Golden Wonders, mastering the slow tock
of darts and billiard tick, protégé of their chalk subtracted
lunchtimes until you pitched up kissing the vicar's niece who
bewildered you with her gusseted etiquettes and the eternal
disco truths of Donna Summer, moaning through the cider in
tongues of Moroder, trapped between straw bales with martyred
arses hastening each cautious impregnation. And now you're squeezed
between a mortgage and an overdraft as fear marches on the backs of ants
through every crack into your family home. You're ticket number 109 on banking
death row yet what terrifies you is not the cliff's edge but having nowhere left to fall.

DOWN AMONG THE SHEDMEN

For the Shedmen of Wandsworth
it's the month of great hunkering.
Winter, grey and skinny, loiters
like a hoodie round the corner
with his pisshead mate Christmas.

The Shedmen fist their mugs of tea
as sweet and brown as the allotment
where they sit on good spade days
hunched in busted plastic chairs
banished from marital patios.

The Shedmen mustn't grumble.
Between retreat and armistice
they hint at bold escape plans
in their voluntary Colditz
watched by poplars still as sentries.

The Shedmen poke the idle smoke
from bonfires that can't be arsed
to rage or dance flamenco,
stoking up dreams that smoulder
in the green damp snapping fire.

Yet still they believe - in rhubarb,
swiss chard and monogamy,
folding each sodden day back
into itself with loam and hoe
in sombre geometry.

RIVER LEE FISH SONG

A million small acts of light
jig across the deeper channel,
splitting Cork like a tuning fork
between the Dominican Church
and the black-cap Calvinist gulls
damning the blushes of salmon.
Downstream a dark head juts up,
snorts, wheezes and scuppers along
whiskered like a Victorian gent
who learned to swim from diagrams
with a cumbersome contraption
propelling his bellyness onward.
The lady with too many bags
for a Sunday and bobble hat
embroidered with golden bees
casts a sprat down from the bridge.
The old seal humps to catch it
then plunges to run the thrum
of cables in the winding tide
where they play rusty covers
of Happiness and other hits
from the lost albums of industry.

FISHSPEAK

By their slow openings
and silken, hookable lips
you know which poets are fish,
eyes applied sideways
spying two worlds at one time
while sliding between both
like it was the only path.

Because their memory silts
as quick as hour-glass sand,
they go from egg to bones
in one adjectival blur,
surviving without verbs
perfectly incomplete.
They trail tropic plumes
glittering with nostalgia
and other parasites
while a sediment of nouns
turns to rasping coral
under their fancy fins.

That's why poet fish are cursed.
Should you manage to translate
any of their moby dickery
you'll never want to put one
in your mouth again.

THE BOOK OF UNDERILLUMINATED MANUSCRIPTS

He had noted the lack in the rat skin of the dead.
There was no light at the end of the world,
just many other worlds all ending on the same page.
The only blaze he saw glazed the feasted faces
of the brothers goosing the pickings of the poor.

So he packed pumice, chalk, stylus, vellum, inks and
made for a pathless forest which welcomed the sun
only in winter as sap slept and clouds grazed the land.
In a pit, he built a hut, sprang traps, drank slate water.
In the undivided darkness, he started on Genesis.

The wordless couple in the walled garden of shades.
A knowledge tree knobbed with bitter white buds,
leafless, its poisoned roots writhing with serpents.
The Flood and its Ark, humped like the other whales,
barren islands in a night sea awaiting the moonlit dove.

Humans stacking up a charnel house into the heavens
to blacken the face of God and have their tongues
divided forever from the truth and from friendship.
Pharohs brooding in their living tombs before rains
poured grey pocks of pestilence upon them.

When he came to render a rainbow coat for Joseph,
he confronted the gift of pure love from father to son:
how it could not pale with Divine rage, pride or jealousy.
So he pitched his book into the fire's dying embers
to wonder at the colour of the simplest miracle.

LOOK AT THOSE CAVEMEN GO

Try not to hear crumpling steel as boots press
into snow, pricking along the valley
from the stone bridge like poor double stitching
pulling the woollen sky much too tight.

You brush through the brambles and ice brocades
past roofless arches at the sulphur baths,
its bruised stucco sprayed with pink fascisms,
to where the other mammals stand sentry.

A stream has followed you round the headland,
veined under the frozen skin of the land.
If a traveller ever walks across Mars
and listens hard, this how Life will sound.

MY BRITISH TEETH

Before the extraction, she had to smash it in three pieces.
Each shard she withdrew, bloody and sharp from the drool,
ranging them on the tray like Boadicea's arrowheads.

With each dental invasion, my mouth became an atrocity
from a barnacled Martello molar at the back,
to the gleaming high rise implants that never settled right.

When the wedding snapper said cheese my lips drew back
and said aggressive chimp in alpha male stand off.
Not what the bride's father considered civil or eugenic.

In a moonlit defection my tongue found an American mouth
for a year or two until her mocking incisors withdrew.
Now it prods about existentially, like Eno in Tescos.

Maybe I'll follow Grandpa Tommy with his clacking palate.
When he yawned his maw became The Scream by Munch,
his loose choppers as adrift as a gull in the ocean dark.

He left them grinning from the whisky glass by his coffin
before they planted him under a marble headstone,
part of a set made for somebody else on the NHS.

MANPRINTS

Dad's shoes guard the back door
empty of him but walking me back
through our decades of departings.
The leather's stretched to its limits;
without feet, they make coracles,
notched and ribbed and thonged
like Bronze Age getaway vehicles.
Hammered by a thousand marches
across vast and sodden land masses
his soles have vulcanised into flat fish
with brass eyes and twine laces.
He was never a "slip-on" kind of guy.
Just like my lad whose school shoes
have hollowed into leaky barges
steering their pilot into reed beds
and volery round the river's bend.
On the clover verge beside the path
I notice my own boot's ousey press,
between a duck and a hand grenade.
And you ask why we waste our time
trying to find wings we left behind.

CHOCOLATE

The miracle will happen
at human melting point.
Brittle slate will turn bitter sweet
along your tongue's equator.
Your pink taste buds will darken
with the rub of salt and guilt.
Part of you will liquify.
Praise be those brand name Quakers
who shook before Jehovah
the better our teeth should rot
than our shrivelling livers
tempt us far from temperance.
We cannot sin together
but at least accept this square,
snapped from its lunar wrapping,
as the closest we will come
to suck-it-and-see salvation.
I promise not to watch.
Everyone loves chocolate.

THE LAMINATIONS

Amid the crashing,
you missed next door's soul
shooting free of rubble
deflected off the skip
with a clunking blue flash
towards Croydon.
Perhaps it meant to go elsewhere.
They stack salvaged bricks
in wobbly columns out back
like a garden in Pompei.
A pyre gyres plastic black
cremating many decades
of botchery by innocents
with hammers and laminates,
as cheap as chipboard.
Into the woebegone lawn
an Armitage Shanks
sinks like a senator's bust
once roost to a hundred bums,
from old readers of Priestly
to the fire eaters of Nigella.
The new owners look on,
faces sharp as smart phones
planning the basement gym
and a rooftop jacuzzi
for the angels.

THE IKEA DICTIONARY OF KRAPP
(inspired by a chair called Knutstorp)

TJORVALV.	Disposable pressure cooker
PNUFF.	Eco-friendly balsa wood fuses
KNOBFLOP.	Armchair commode
JOLIPOK.	Human shaped cushion
GORBAL.	Portable urinal for hall or landing
GRUNTIG.	Joke covered tea towel
WUPSALA.	Diagonal bookshelves
DRAKFLO.	Self-draining salad bowl
SMEGBLURT.	Goat wool fertility blanket
TORPOST.	A2 framed poster of Thor
WODENPOST.	Stake for the garden
LEDHORN.	Nuclear pencil sharpener
NEKKA.	Domestic Office axe
NEKKAKA.	Double headed axe (out of stock)
STEWLSLIK.	Day-Glo disembowelling tool
THRAKULL.	Enamel breastplate
ROKBOM.	Indoor sacrificial barbeque
BEKA.	Blood carrying beaker set
BURBL.	Ancestral shrine with fondue
AHA	Non-toxic war paint
SEEVOLVO.	50 person dragon ship
SAGA	Life insurance for the over 50's
STOBLAST.	Single village explosives kit
KOMKOM.	Pillage assistance alarm
HAKTI	Bleached pine limb bunker
NOBELO.	Head storage vessel (pack of 10)
DANGLU.	Flat pack teak veneer gallows
FLAR.	Cremation salts
MULCHEE.	Collapsible grave shovel
TRISTING.	Funerary hand towel
BLOTASH.	Votive offerings, assorted
PARKING.	24 hours free
CHILDCARE.	
MEATBALLS.	